BEASTS OF NALUNGA

Jack Mapanje is Malawi's best-known poet, linguist, editor and human rights activist. Formerly head of department of English in the University of Malawi, he was imprisoned by dictator Hastings Kamuzu Banda and his inner circle, largely for his radical poetry and views. He stayed at the notorious Mikuyu Prison for 3 years, 7 months, 16 days and more than 12 hours, without trial or charge.

His books of poetry include *Of Chameleons and Gods* (1981) and *The Chattering Wagtails of Mikuyu Prison* (1993) from Heinemann, and from Bloodaxe Books: *Skipping Without Ropes* (1998), *The Last of the Sweet Bananas: New & Selected Poems* (2004) and *Beasts of Nalunga* (2007). He co-edited *Oral Poetry from Africa: an anthology* (Longman, 1983), *Summer Fires: New Poetry of Africa* (Heinemann, 1983), and *The African Writers' Handbook* (African Book Collective, 1999); and edited *Gathering Seaweed: African prison writing* (Heinemann, 2002).

He has taught at the University of Leeds; held writing residencies at the University of Leiden (The Netherlands), University College Cork, St Anthony's College, Oxford, The Open University and the University of Warwick. After spending three years as poet in residence for the Wordsworth Trust at Dove Cottage, Grasmere, Cumbria, where most of the poems in *Beasts of Nalunga* were written, he took up the post of Senior Lecturer in Creative Writing in the School of English, the University of Newcastle upon Tyne. Mapanje lives in York with his family.

JACK MAPANJE

BEASTS OF NALUNGA

BLOODAXE BOOKS

ISBN: 978 1 85224 771 3

First published 2007 by
Bloodaxe Books Ltd,
Highgreen,
Tarset,
Northumberland NE48 1RP.

www.bloodaxebooks.com
For further information about Bloodaxe titles
please visit our website or write to
the above address for a catalogue.

Bloodaxe Books Ltd acknowledges
the financial assistance of
Arts Council England, North East.

Cover design: Neil Astley & Pamela Robertson-Pearce.

Cover printing: J. Thomson Colour Printers Ltd, Glasgow.

Printed in Great Britain by
Bell & Bain Limited, Glasgow, Scotland.

To my family and friends:

Resilience is like a swallow,
It swoops and turns across
Mountains, valleys, waters
Evading the sharp beaks of
Killer-hawks until it perches
On fragrant tree branches.

NEW PROVERB

ACKNOWLEDGEMENTS

Grateful thanks are due to the editors of the following publications where some of the poems first appeared: *Edinburgh Review*, *The Shop* (Ireland), *Stand*, *37th Poetry International Festival programme* (Rotterdam) and *A Winter Garland* (The Wordsworth Trust, 2003). Several poems were previously published, some in earlier versions, in *The Last of the Sweet Bananas: New & Selected Poems* (Bloodaxe Books/Wordsworth Trust, 2004).

Thanks also to producers of poetry programmes on BBC Radio 3 and 4, where some of the poems were commissioned or first discussed. The "writers group" of colleagues in the School of English, University of Newcastle upon Tyne deserves mention for their critical comments on the raw form of some of these pieces, and special thanks to Desmond Graham and David Kerr for helping me tighten this and that – the shortcomings in these final versions are due to my stubbornness. Neil Astley and his colleagues at Bloodaxe Books deserve a special hug for their encouragement and fine production. Financial assistance from the K. Blundell Trust, the Authors' Foundation and Arts Council England gave me a peace of mind that helped to complete and restructure this book; I am deeply indebted to them.

CONTENTS

OF VAMPIRES AND SILENCES OF HOME

Beasts of Nalunga

I

No, I never thought I'd
return to them so early
but beasts of Nalunga
have a mind of their own
that draws out the most
tenacious in us within
their temporal spirals,
trying our temper and
tempting our faith. Our
antediluvian sages were
right to consider them
too stubborn; for beasts
of Nalunga have legs that
won't lift, eyes with mind-
boggling cataracts, ears
which won't hear, flesh
and bones that won't feel –
they are most eloquent
when the gods conspire
with despots to suppress
people's inventive ways.

II

Beasts of Nalunga seize
their time when the land
is dry and cave panthers
rip out frogs that might
shelter them; torrential rains
are then unleashed dragging
away fire places, gobbling
up jars, pots, ladles, hoes,
calabashes, sending homes
tumbling down canyons,
swirling with people's cattle,
sheep, goats, dogs, chicken –
the lot – as men, women,
children fumble, knock
about, forever sashaying
to nondescript labyrinths
en route to far-off waters
and lakes, seas and oceans.

III

When their moment comes
beasts of Nalunga respect
no one – the young, aged,
the poor must all churn in
the gushing brown currents
gurgling down inscrutable
pathways to the rhythmic
thunderbolts that consume
whatever gets in their way;
but beasts of Nalunga are
at their most loquacious
veiled as vampires that suck
ordinary people's blood at
night, often with intricate
intravenous tubing, leaving
behind invisible blemishes
as people flee their homes.

IV

Ask whoever cares to know,
ask whoever wants to remember,
ask Chilobwe, Mchesi, other
township or country chiefs,
they'll show you the blood
their despotic regime once
swapped for apartheid gold
wherever the Young Pioneers
with their 'spearhead' this
and 'spearhead' that stood
sentry. As for today's born-
again Young Democrats ask
Chiwere, cheSomba or other
chiefs, they'll testify to blood-
letting rituals that have come
with the new liberties which
other beasts summon in order
to wheedle western food-aid
and beat eternal famines,
malaria, AIDS, plagues that
our western pharmaceuticals,
patented by their beasts of
IMF, World Bank, forever
profit from, whichever way
our politicians may dispute
the origins of our burdens.

V

It's after they've drained
the people's blood that
the lion heads, rhinoceros
trunks and hyena hinds –
the sphinxes we call beasts
of Nalunga – prowl about
the land marauding like
rabid monsters, maiming.
And no guns, not even
game rangers' guns; no
voices, not even ancestral
voices, no police bullets,
no army bombs, no Young
Pioneer *machete* or Young
Democrat *phangas*, nothing
but nothing beats beasts
of Nalunga; stab, hack or
shoot them, no blood will
splatter nor is their DNA
detectable; whatever you
take them, however you
see them, the brutes will
not shy away, for beasts
of Nalunga are cyclic sagas
of people besotted by wars,
battles, tyrants, plagues.

VI

And when riddlers call
beasts of Nalanga spirits
of the innocent that our
hit squads 'accidentalised'
once, now seeking peace
for their mangled bodies
with today's dispensation;
when our narrators today,
poets tomorrow remember
to restore the victims of
beasts of Nalunga to their
rightful pages in the nation's
history, let these and other
singers craft the truths we
were silent about for fear of
death; maybe it's right that
a few riddlers remember

the ad hoc mat-coffins that
took some mangled bodies
past ordinary doors, when
they should have gone out
to their impromptu graves
past windows, according to
tattoos from the medicine
men and women who gave
them new lease of life; may-
be singers are duty-bound
to remember the coffins that
should not have been buried
at gun point, or carcasses of
the 'politicals' who did not
deserve to dissolve in basins
of sulphuric acid at Malawi
Young Pioneer bases, when
it was a crime to shed tears
for family branded 'rebels'.

VII

So, when the wizards and
witches practise their rites
openly, given the liberties
we enjoy; when the satanic
disciples insist on pinning
down beasts of Nalunga
each into their frames as
as patented by World Bank,
IMF and other pecuniary
beasts; when we wish these
beasts bound up hand and
foot, and left stark naked on
mountain tops, for vultures
to feast on, as fated by our
ancient rituals; even when
city, town, township taxis
take beasts of Nalunga for
their life despot returned
from hellfire to taunt easy
up country people, replete
with spirits of his Young
Pioneers, Womens League
and dancing the big dance at
their hero's open air theatre
of barbed wire cemetery –

indeed, when the country's
criers scour the rift valleys,
cliffs and mountain ranges
pulling their nets of twine,
each hoping to catch beasts
of Nalunga of their desire –
nobody but nobody knows
where the beasts of Nalunga
come from, where they are
headed and what they really
are; the truth must surely be:
when our temporal spirals
have done their final round,
we'll find beasts of Nalunga
lurking here, lurking there,
lurking even in you and me.

Rested Among Fellow Hyenas, Finally?

(for David Kerr)

So the undertakers have buried
Their lion of the nation for life
Among the hyenas he ridiculed
At political rallies once? Have

They embalmed their notable
In his waistcoat, striped dark
Suit, bowler hat, overcoat and
The sunglasses that screened

Our endless anxieties too? Did
The woodpeckers, squirrels, cats
And snakes spit in disbelief as
The fly whisk which swiped their

Laughter shut was placed on
His right – lest another mosquito
Zang past to upset his eternal
Glory? And did the gravediggers

Afterwards truly return to harvest
His flaming garlands for their
Next highest bidding client, one
By one, dancing their dance of

Witches as the palm leaf flames
Flattered in the dark? Did they
Ask about his lavish banquets,
The farms his hangers-on will

Scramble over? What welcome did
His Young Pioneer invented rebels
Give him on arrival? Did they ask
How it felt to be finally there, alone?

And were those battles he fought
To become another Almighty God
Worth spilling his people's blood
For, eventually? Will taxis really

Show us the solitary barbed wire
Cemetery where his rabid hyenas
Gather at night stomping about,
Foaming for his bones – glory be!

Henry Masauko Chipembere's Mango Tree at Mtundu, cheChiwaya's

The fig tree at Mtundu, cheChiwaya's was
robust, dynamic once – political arena, court,
market; chiefs and their elders chewed our
cases in subtle riddles, proverbs, narratives
there, fishmongers milling about bamboo and
reed stalls, trading sun-dried *utaka, usipa, nchila,*
zisawasawa, mcheni for salt, sugar, beads;
women in cheerful calico offered spirited prices
for their sweet brew, babies on backs munching
banana bread baked in banana leaves. And
this mango tree, this arch rebel standing tall
beside the fig tree at Mtundu, cheChiwaya's
hasn't it weathered ruthless Young Pioneer
butts, Youth League lashes these years? And
when figs and mangoes, finally fall to earth,
like their rebel hero, will swallows swoop
and turn to gathering clouds and whirlwind,
promising another bitter-sweet fruitfulness?

utaka, usipa, nchila, zisawasawa, mcheni: Lake Malawi is known for having the largest variety of fresh water fish in the world, these are some of them.

Silences Surrounding Mama's Unfinished City Flats, 2002

When His Excellency the Life
President and his crocodiles were
beaten and new liberties won and
people began again to talk openly
how the despot's mama suddenly
produced the certificate of her
secret marriage to him, hiding his
death certificate with his millions
scattered in world capital banks,
the taxis kindly drove us to another
drama of mama's capital city flats
that people daren't mention for
fear another ritual death might meet
whoever uncovered the secret.

When we saw grass and bush
growing in mama's unfinished
flats, we feared the anger this
curious generation would suffer
when the silences we begot
in our hideous images are exposed –
won't the youths rush down our
streets like riots some day? But
the taxis assured us: indeed it'd
be foolish to count on generations
of youths who might in time detect
the awkward questions only public
houses dared to whisper once –

'If you were Life President's
private secretary, permanent
mistress, his official hostess,
the mama, with brutal uncles,
brothers, sisters, cronies and,
earning a modest civil service
salary, would you be the sole
owner of one of capital city's
housing estates, with its super
stores, maize, tobacco, animal
farms blossoming everywhere
and those unfinished city flats –
without bullying the Treasury

on behalf of the Life President,
which contractors should be
offered the tenders for national
development projects as you
all gazed in petrified silences?'

Of course, we stroked our chins,
whispering: 'Indeed how foolish
we had been to believe they'd
all be gone the taxis that still
remembered how we bullied
the Treasury on behalf of His
Excellency the Life President!'

This Grain That Keeps Leaving Its Silos

If you've been watching stories of bags
upon bags of maize disappearing from
people's silos, without trace, into garages

of politicians and their bureaucrats only
to be sold back at pitiless profits to dying
up country people, or across the borders;

if you care to remember histories of these
silos – how those American drones spying
from above almost blew them up once

'thinking' they were another Cold War
nuclear plant from the other side; if images
of distended men, women and children

have moved you, and perhaps for once,
you considered them just another batch
of our endless African jokes gone sour –

I suggest you watch the state president's
governors, who, though elected to supplant
the last of our despots, continue to build

barbed wire fences that safeguard their
bellies, relatives, authority from the truth,
drenching fig trees all over the land in

fierce storms about the people's universal
fertilisers, starter packs, their aged treadle-
pumps, the grain sold across the borders.

And should your conscience fray, impotent, as
blighted bellies gather the last green elephant
grass to fight the famines the politicians deny,

engage hope where it is silent, craft on those
riddles, proverbs, narratives your sages in their
copious voices showed you many years ago;

sing, even cry yourselves sore, until maybe
your tales stop the pledges crossing borders,
or the people's grain disappearing from silos!

Prisons That Still Choke Us Cold

I remember joking about the prisons
We'd be carrying wherever we strayed
After our three and a half years ordeal.
We must convert Mikuyu Prison into
A museum, with photographs of all
'Politicals' in their huge unshaven beards
And moustaches, their presumed crimes
And the years they were incarcerated
All meticulously inscribed below their
Photographs, 'After our new liberties
Have been won,' we said. Indeed, didn't
Mikuyu Prison become a museum for
Ten years, though without photographs,
Names, or cases of those incarcerated
For nothing there, and no curator.
                                        And today you
Are telling me Mikuyu Prison is back
To prison and Maula Prison choking
With criminals from the melting pot
You've won for the entire region? And
At night *nyapalas* still shout 'All Turn'
And all prisoners turn on the other side
At once, crushing on each other's torsos,
In heaps worse than the sardines on
Decks of slave ships years ago? What
Of other ever-choking prisons: Zomba
Central, Chichiri, Dzeleka, secluded
Nsanje; what of the extra prison each
District opened for the despot and his
Coterie instead of schools, clinics, roads?
Dear spirits of fire rains, winds, where
Are the prayers that calmed harsh waters
To liberate your people from bondage?

Another Tomb 40 Years On

Was it for erecting this marble
Mausoleum for Hastings Banda
That Dunduzu Kaliu Chisiza was
Accidentalised at Thondwe Bridge;
Henry Masauko Chipembere
Poisoned under the convenience
Of diabetes in America; Yatuta
Chisiza at Mwanza fell with his
Batch of tough rebels, the Young
Pioneers forcing us to view their
Mangled bodies at Queen Elizabeth
Hospital mortuary to scare us into
Submission; Augustine Bwanausi
In Lusaka car-crashed; Attati
Mpakati at Stanley Hotel, Harare,
Assassinated; John Msonthi for
His radiant translation of Banda's
Speeches and Chidzanja Nkhoma
For his enviable central region
Following, both 'jujued'; Medson
Evance Silombera, Kumpyelula
Kanada both publicly hanged;
Gomile Kuntumanji buried like
Another rabid dog for Chilobwe
Murders Banda conceived; Aaron
Gadama, Dick Matenje, David
Chiwanga and Twaibu Sangala
Clubbed to death to protect our
Despot's inner circle; Mkwapatira
Mhango and his family of nine
Bombed in Lusaka for exposing
CCAM lies; Orton Ching'oli
Chirwa done at Zomba Central
Prison for fear he'd lead the new
Liberties about to be truly won –
What shameless, needless, endless
Martyrs this nation boasts! What
Hundreds of thousands of freedom
Fighters accidentalised, imprisoned,
Exiled, more than 30 years, who
Merit finer marble mausoleums!

A Million Ways of Re-burying a Despot

(after Paul Farley)

There are ways of re-burying a despot that
don't need a mausoleum; a contraption of

grass, reed, bamboo; a puddle of a grave like
the ones his crocodiles dug for his presumed

political enemies, and the vultures can handle
the rest. And if his millions were the problem,

the millions his self-appointed heirs changed
his will for, when they saw him gasping for life,

there are nobler ways of disposing of a despot's
millions that don't need a mausoleum; skeletal

up country people dying, or thriving on wild
grass – didn't his crocodiles gather his millions

from people's loin-cloth purses they forced as
'presents for your Life President!' at his mass

rallies? There are ways of remembering a despot
that don't need a mausoleum for reconciliation;

forgetting the livid open letters you wrote about
the silences his inner circle imposed; hammering

them on tree trunks; scattering copies at markets,
churches, public houses and dancing arenas at

night; thwarting his security officers; until his
referendum brought you promises of another

life; there must be a million ways of re-burying
the despot that don't need this mausoleum!

When You've Never Lived under a Despot

When you've never lived under
a despot admit it, his minions never
made you dance in the flaming heat
nor forced you to offer your last cow,
goat, sheep, chicken, egg or coin
hidden in the loin-cloth purse
around your waist.

When you've never lived under
a despot concede, you do not know
the deadly concertos of his dancing witches:
the Women's League, Youth League,
Young Pioneers who whipped
up his support.

When you've never lived under
the despot's minions confess, you will
never feel the hit squads that bumped off
the political rebels they fashioned
for their president for life, forever
poisoning the nation.

When you've been the despot's
self-appointed heir, henchman and
hanger-on accept, you'll never hear
the silences that slit the throats of
Life President's suspected traitors
as ruthlessly as they slashed their
fruitful 'rebel' maize gardens,

burning down 'disloyal' grain-bursting
granaries for exposing their silences.
When you've never truly lived under
a despot and his ferocious dogsbodies
acknowledge, otherwise you'll never
spot the larger plot.

Prayers for Paramount Sages

'Dear spirits of our fathers and
mothers, these spirals of denial world
without end, what paramount sages will
you send now to repair the invisibility of
your ordinary people, forever suffering,
forever dying, whatever brand of
political regime takes the arena?

And dear youths who must know our
time in these never-ending liberation
struggles is done, why must you still clutch
at the tail-end of western gimmicks going:
big brother this, celebrity that, idol this,
reality that, hand driven radios, hand
wound computers – all purporting to heal

the pain we invent for up country people?

And these red, black and white ribbons,
these bands, these 'make poverty history'
doggerels, when will human life without
a God, without a plot, translate? The reality
is the west never fulfils whatever it pledges;
their global village was never meant for you;
the west wants you wherever you are forever!

Why, therefore, oh Christ, why do you
still gaze elsewhere for answers here? Why
don't you see there will be no better time
for you to enter the arena with finer voices
and thereby perhaps give the ordinary
people the dignity they have
always deserved?'

OF HOMES WEIRDLY SWEET

The Magpies of New Earswick

Today, Auntie Mercy calls Yorkshire Spring
Her season of magpies; when the daffodils
And crocuses break out, the magpies hang

About, watching the blackbirds as they
Nest in her loft, waiting on their prey. At
First she thought it another joke to salute

The ominous visitors of her lodgers as
Her neighbour's children did, 'Good
Morning Mr Magpie!' each time the black

And white stripes threatened to strike at
The chicks from her loft. And when
Twigs from their beaks dropped, heaping

At the foot of her door as her blackbirds
Gathered their nest, fouling wall and door,
Auntie Mercy merely mused, 'And how

Clever is that, can't you see the magpies
Of New Earswick biding their time?'
Often she wondered if the magpies came

Here to torment not just her blackbirds
But her too, like Tang Hall youths once,
Throwing their dirt into her chicken stew

When she first crushed there or like those
Cheeky New Earswick children flinging
Conkers at the alien nurse who sauntered

Up and down their street to hospital day
After day when she transferred here; but
These days, when she hears fresh blackbird

Chicks chirruping in her loft and fears for
Another season of magpies that has arrived,
Auntie Mercy has learnt to put her feet up

To her blackbirds' chatter, watching all
The antiques of the magpies. Yesterday
She even laughed when our Kate teased,

'When this massive magpie crossed my path
At my first driving test, didn't I shout, 'Mr
Magpie!' and indeed fail the test?' Next

Year, the children and I want to take Auntie
Mercy to St James's Park, we think she's ready
To watch the Gunners play real Magpies.

The Minster Inn, York

When Robinson Crusoe grabbed his fishing tackle
Hopped onto the driftwood tied tight to the grass

Thicket of the lagoon and floated away, singing
About the gods of tilapia and mudfish which had

Steered his life hitherto, did he anticipate landing
Among the aliens he'd long feared for rejecting

The cloud upon which other fairies were meant
To flutter? But when he saw the goblins gasping for

Fresh air in their drunken cellars, too ashamed
To invoke the gods they'd long shunned, Crusoe

Bloated his familial proverb: 'when handshakes go
Beyond the elbow, brother, move on, before their

Battles begin'; yet pondering the worms for bait
Strewn among the childhood fish traps of home

And watching the imminent 'glories' of their New
Millennium, Crusoe began to dither, so, choosing

The corner pedestal of the city's Public House, he
Too carelessly burped, 'I'm only here for the beer!'

Fleeting Child of the 3-Day Week

Hang on, Mister, I too was here when
The Winter of Discontent broke out
And London bin men let London stink.

I was here when 3-day week closed our
Libraries at 5.30 each day and my friend
And I rushed for Goodge Street Tube

Station, headed for the Circle Line that
Twirled us round, round, round, round –
'Studying in the round' we christened

It – until 'All Change' brought us back
To Lillian Penson Hall to watch Trevor
McDonald's ITV *News at 10.* When those

In high places insisted on their lives being
Covered but let Green Goddesses lumber
Awkwardly up people's streets to quench

Their fires, refusing to see their poodles'
Muck on the asphalt, I noted the jokes.
Our Commonwealth numbers in Sussex

Gardens voted in Paddington's Labour
MP too! And when the Brixton-Wood
Green riots blazed, they stopped my car

At Tally Ho to hear if I spoke Birmingham –
Where they thought the riots originated.
Besides, you've never watched Notting

Hill Carnival from Chepstow Road nor
Published poems in Alan Ross's *London*
Magazine – with real poets! Where were

You when they knocked out Red Ken for
The socialist GLC they invented? What have
You done to dub me economic migrant?

What do you know about the economics
Migrants suffer? By your piddling dossier
You have not even run from IRA Tube

Station bomb scares! Get real then, if you
Are truly serious about your global village,
This is no fleeting child of your 3-day week!

After Celebrating Our Asylum Stories at West Yorkshire Playhouse, Leeds

So, define her separately,
She's not just another
Castaway washed up your
Rough seas like driftwood,
It's the nameless battles
Your sages burdened her
People that broke her back;
Define him differently,
He's not another squirrel
Ousted from your poplars,
It's the endless cyclones,
Earthquakes, volcanoes,
Floods, mud and dust that
Drafted him here; define
Them warmly, how could
Your economic émigré queue
At your job centres day after
Day? If you must, define us
Gently, how do you hope
To see the tales we bear
When you refuse to hear
The whispers we share?

The Seashells of Bridlington North Beach

(for Mercy Angela)

She hated anything caged, fish particularly,
Fish caged in glass boxes, ponds, whatever;

'Reminds me of prisons and slavery,' she said;
So, when first she caught the vast green view

Of Bridlington North Beach shimmering that
English summer day, she greeted the sight like

A Sahara girl on parched feet, cupping, cupping,
Cupping the water madly, laundering her palms,

Giggling and laughing. Then rubbing the hands
On her skirt, she threw her bottom on the sandy

Beach and let the sea breathe in and out on her
As she relaxed her crossed legs – 'Free at last!'

She announced to the beach crowds oblivious;
And as the seascape rallied and vanished at her

Feet, she mapped her world, 'The Netherlands
We visited must be here; Norway, Sweden there;

Beyond that Russia!' Then gathering more sea-
shells and selecting them one by one, she turned

To him, 'Do you remember eating porridge from
Beach shells once?' He nodded, smiling at another

Memory of the African lakes they were forced to
Abandon. 'Someday, perhaps I'll take that home

To celebrate!' She said staring into the deep sea.
Today, her egg-like pebbles, her pearls of seashells

Still sparkle at the windowsill; her wishes still ring,
'Change regularly the water in the receptacles to

Keep the pebbles and seashells shining – you'll
See, it's a lot healthier than feeding caged fish!'

No Swearing, Please, We've Children About

Should you, therefore, perhaps feel a little incarcerated,
Should GNER carriages start jerking, squeaking, shrieking

To a halt, then picking up speed for the umpteenth time;
Should the impassive passengers in time begin to twitch

At the official voices piping through, lavishly apologising
About the delay, do not despair; imagine the explosion

That might have been near the gas station, if the fire
Had flared beyond repair as you screeched from another

Reading at Stirling University. And forget the fellow
fidgeting with his crossword beside you, forget the lass

Babbling on her mobile – chilling out on her party last night!
When GNER finally squeals at 'Darlington Station Stop'

Another train will be waiting, as sterner reminders bellow
About taking your baggage before you transfer to platform 4

But watch, watch when the reality eventually strikes home,
Watch the passengers suddenly ablaze and damning this,

Damning that, rubbishing this, rubbishing GNER's selfish
Directors, invoking the 'f' words you never thought their

Crosswords would imbibe; and when you 'settle' in your
New seat, do not let the lady beside you hot up about her

Booking arrangements disrupted, lest you miss the bigger
Picture: 'No swearing, please, we have children about!'

The Grumpy Old Hippopotami of Tala Game Reserve, Kwazulu, Natal, 1999

(for Matthew Sweeney)

Tell them to emulate the ostriches who accost their
Snoops by attenuating their necks, walking tall on

The brown sedges, grasses and ferns of Tala Game
Reserve; tell them to watch the giraffes who peak

Their ears above the acacia treetops then, unruffled
By their own majesty, slouch their welcome, nibbling

At the little green leaves between the sharp thorns.
Why don't they delight like the secretary birds who,

After stroking each other, their ponytails flaunting
In the winter breeze, draw out their wings, fly-dancing

And mock-fighting their aerial display before us; why
Don't they marvel at the black rhinoceroses that block our

Tracks, refusing to begrudge us the spectacle of their mum's
Protracted piercing piss? Tell them even hippopotami

Can master the craft of the resplendent wildebeest,
The nimble antelope and agile zebra; and insist they are

Mere hippopotami blown into the lake by the burden
Of chance, if they want to get on here, they will have

To fluster at whatever bird picks their noses next time,
They'll have to grunt at the interlopers who want progress

On their estate – if it's apartheid they still bemoan, tell
Them, 'Forget it, the brute will never come back!'

The Patron of Jubilee 2000

(Celebrating the Life of Mwalimu Julius Nyerere of Tanzania, 19 April 2000, London)

I should have engaged your mind
In your modest village house where
The Kilimanjaro beacon shone through

The political fevers of the Great Rift
Valley; not in my undergraduate
Essays on dead empires and stubborn

Despots, along dusty nondescript
Corridors of campuses beside another
Independence Arch of minor rift

Valleys; for, when the leopard leapt
I beheld the foreign foxes panic at
The contested ground; I spied Black

Ant creep up elephant's ears and sting,
Sting, sting until the beast of apartheid
Dropped dead. Our very flamingos

Peeped through the spy-holes of their
Prisons as your People's Women's League
Pleaded with their despot's official Mama

To get her to break the chains around
Our fragile bones. And what images,
What rhythmic tapestry, what symbols

Haunt your Swahili *Julius Caesar* and
The Merchant of Venice! No wonder
This gazelle still enthuses over your

Ujamaa this *ujamaa* that mostly *ujamaa*
About the liberation of the entire Great Rift
Valley. But gazing from your haven now,

Does Black Ant blush as grasshoppers
Fumble over present global injustices?
No matter, patron of peace, *harambee!*

Letter to Landeg White in Portugal, October 2001

The sycamores and poplars you abandoned
have begun to cast their brown along the cold
pavements, soon the soggy leaves will bring

the electric trains to their knees, shaming our
advanced civilisation, and the charcoal grey
avenues will shudder under the dull English

winter. Yorkshire supermarkets are already
haggling over prices of computer gimmicks
for the children at Halloween, Guy Fawkes,

Christmas; another Mama and Papa on TV
will doubtless stammer over the cheap crackers
that blew up their child's fingers – threatening

the foreign dealers with the summons! Indeed
the New Millennium has been and gone, who-
ever said eat and drink, the end's nigh, will

have to read the signs of the times again. But
how's it with you there, won't the sardines too
reduce to the famous 9/11 binary opposition?

Driving along the narrow lanes of Yorkshire
dales today, alone, I remembered the pheasants
we hunted in your rusty Nissan, weaving down

God's colourful canvas spanning the land –
stuff Tesco's frozen stuffing, let's hunt
fresh birds to celebrate our liberation from

The African crocodiles, we thought, but not
a pheasant's wretched feather crossed our
lanes then nor today! My dear friend, don't

you sometimes wonder at the wisdom of these
places we are forever trading – you among smoking
Portuguese grapes gathering another nest, yours

truly still spelling his name amidst these mouldy
hedgerows? When will our grand rodent show
up – if only to tone up God Almighty's dales!

The Wedding of Jacarandas

(for Judith & Nicholas, January 2005)

'When the crocodiles of home
forced us unto the foreign lands
we are forever adopting, they hoped
we'd never discover how they blew
their noses above the rough waters
and believed we'd never again check
our fish traps for glistening tilapia
or sing and dance to our big dance –
but they were, as always, wrong!
For, today, as your shades of Zomba
jacarandas blossom, dear Judith,
happily wedded to shades of Masaka
jacarandas, dear Nicholas; as Christ
the King Catholic Church brushes
aside the dry brown dust of Kampala
city, my dear children, today you
shame mum and me for bothering
about the beasts of home when we
should have been dancing all along.

'Do not falter then, dear daughter,
we, your own blood, could not
have married you off to a pack of
stubborn wolves; and do not fear,
dear son, we could not have brought
you into another uncaring village
kraal! Remember what love, what
pledges and promises brought us
here, remember the coffee beans
the elders from both sides cracked
in Kampala and Masaka, remember
how we broke the delicious chicken
baked in banana leaf satchels, how
the treasured friends who flew with
us saw the source of River Nile and
crossed the Equator myth – catching
the water twirling left, twirling right,
standing still – all for your wedlock.

'Do not forget, therefore, to bring
that golden shield of smile, love,
prayer and caring, upon which your
jacarandas were raised; let the delicate
shades of lilac you grew up on be
your armour to confront the tough
beetles you encounter in the lands
you are forever adopting; may that
ancestral cloud which suddenly broke
into rare showers on that dry and
hazy Masaka sky when we arrived
and curiously haloed your heads
as we parted, forever hug your lilac
dreams, with our eternal blessing!'

On Your Glorious Years, Neil Smith

(20 September 2006)

Dear Neil, as we commemorate your
Glorious years in linguistics today,
I remember when first I entered
UCL; dazzled by fresh smelling
Trees and mazes of lambda operators
On white leaves, you said, simply,
'Relax', their eminencies in linguistics
Are only another bunch of ingenious
Mortals like you and me, then you
Proceeded to map out the human
Face to the gammas and betas. Today,
As we celebrate your life in linguistics,
Accept our appreciation of the career
Of a brilliant teacher, researcher,
Supervisor and tireless linguist; these
Lines are not just for that friend
Who often offered a bob or two
To troubled students to have their
Dissertations properly bound, which
Goes without saying, consider this
Rather, as you might that minimalist
Shrine that maximally explained our
Mutual fascination with language;
This is our humble tribute to that
Robust mind, forever young, forever
Forbidding, forever furnishing fresh
Minds with tough probing, not only
To feed the starving people of our
World, though that was built in too,
But more like freeing the world's
Caged, passing on that singular hope,
That confidence which would rescue
Turtles stranded on their backs on
Far-flung shores. Today, we ask
Only what we've often feared to
Ask: why don't you, now, 'relax'?
Enjoy what you've always wanted
To enjoy, with love and best wishes.

Now That September 11 Should Define Mr Western Civilisation...

(for Sarah Maguire & Saadi Yousef)

I remember being summoned to the British Council Office
Once, back home; I'd got the Commonwealth Scholarship

Bound for the University of London. The British Council
Lady who interviewed us declared, to get the full benefit

Of our studies in metropolitan Britain, we were to listen
Carefully to what she had to say about 'civilisation' – she

Uttered the word as if it were some Country Squire we
Should've been told about at our village school long ago

Or perhaps some gentleman once in a striped suit, bow
Tie, bowler hat, about to sit at table glittering with silver

Cutlery, ready to eat the precious bits and bobs we'd
Never hope to taste. For the lady first fell into a deadly

Trance and, as if in defence of the law she feared we'd
Soon break, stressed, 'If you do not listen, you'll be

Embarrassed when you are invited to civilised homes!'
Meaning where people ate with knives, forks, spoons;

Drank from mugs, cups, glasses; not with hands, sticks
And shards like us drinking from calabashes or gourds!

The lady then showed us how the civilised table was
To be set, with the number of plates minutely spaced

Before us, the knives on the right, the forks on the left,
Knives and spoons on top; which knives went with

Which forks with which food; how we were to begin
With the knives and forks outside the plates and moved

Inside, as it were. 'Quaffing one's drink like American
Cowboys won't do!' She insisted, 'You know what I

Mean!' Of course, we did not know what she meant
Until after entering the British Council Head Office at

65 Davis Street, London, SW1, where the lady's rules
Of engagement drastically changed. Now, weren't we

Urged to, 'Join those Bond Street corner shop queues for
Lunch!' And there, didn't we have to pick our fish 'n' chips

With our flipping fingers, from the cones of London's
Evening Standard Newspaper? Walking down Portobello

Market that evening, didn't we laugh, laugh, laugh until
We broke wind, tears running down cheeks, imagining

The British Council lady's rules so carelessly breached by
Her own mates! That was years ago, though now that 9/11

Defines Lord Western Civilisation of the New Millennium
I thought you might like to hear when first I met the guy!

The Taxis of North Yorkshire

It's how you trusted them so easily
With the story of your life that puzzled,
The way you rushed for the front seat,
Quickly belted up, perhaps apologised
For the slight delay or the Vale of York
Drizzle you brought onto their seats
Before you bombarded them with tales
Of the world you never really shared.
'How dare she walk out on me after
These years?' you began, and chattered
On about the kids, the mortgage, the car
And what to do when she's finally gone.
Often it was the taxis themselves who
Instigated it – 'We are back then, how
Was it where we've been this time?'
And you began your liberal lecture on
Whatever they neither wanted to hear
Nor cared about. Their reaction to their
Radio's social critique was provocative:
'That'll be our learned journalists, at it
Again, the usual crap, if you ask me!'
And titillated you added, 'Don't they
Really believe in the glorious *general public*
They invent and so eloquently speak for!'
About the local elections they knew who
Was coming in and who going out often
Musing, 'What's wrong with politicians,
Why can't they see what we the ordinary
Folk see?' And you rattled your 'whys'
Forever and ever. They had encyclopaedic
Knowledge about who scooped what at
The horse races or football pools, boasted
About the rich and famous they'd driven,
Football hooligans who high-jacked their
Taxis at the weekend binges – 'Oh, how
Those Saturday gate crashers got sick!'
They warned about the cities' dodgy pubs
And alleyways too; but the taxis you so
Dearly loved were at their brightest when
They brandished what they thought you
Needed to think before you offered them
The tip and rolled your baggage home.

The Ballad of *Lady Bibby Renaissance* of Barrow Docks, April 2003

When *Lady Bibby Renaissance* first
Docked at the gateway to the Lake
District, seven years ago, her arrival
Was hailed with bagpipe and string;

She would charm the lakes and waters
With her glittering jewels and pearls
People said; she'd particularly make
A fine five-star hotel drifting on her

200 luxury beds, thought one business
Tycoon – a frill casino on the Irish Sea
That would surpass Las Vegas casinos
More like, challenged another; please

Deck her in rebel colours, give us another
Radio Caroline on The Irish Sea, cried
Mr Dee Jay – indeed *Lady Bibby* was
Everyone's prima donna until the Home

Secretary offered to crown her Britain's
Cutting Edge 'Floating Prison' which'd
Sail in and out of the Irish Channel, free.
When placards against the plan arrived

However, the idea of *Lady B* was shelved,
Until now when the War in Iraq has begun
And threatens to last beyond its remit.
So, we thought we'd bring Abbotsmead

School children to see if *Lady Bibby* could
Mount weapons of mass destruction for
Iraq; but alas, we found her in tattoos,
Rusty tears dripping down her cheeks,

Nor did the ripples painfully smiling at her
Remember whether *Lady B* of Barrow
Docks had come from The Netherlands,
Switzerland or Sweden and why she chose

To idle beside the *Pacific Crane* which once
Commandeered plutonium and other grave
Nuclear wastes to Japan and had to be brought
Back to fulfil other rules of engagement.

Perhaps Abbotsmead school children were
Right – when the War in Iraq is over, *Lady B*
Will feel the blows we dealt her, and crumble –
In protest against the lies we told about her!

Justine Copps of Clapham Village

When you flagged me down
After the roundabout that says
To Kendal 45 miles, I stopped,
In spite of the warnings never
To, however burdened the hikers
Seemed; I guess it was the blinking
Tractors on A59 refusing to give
Way to the madness of my driving
Week after tedious week, from
The Vale of York to the minnows
Of Grasmere – to eke out another
Raw exile – I guess it was fatigue
That did it, when at times, even
The most careful driver felt doped
By the stink of manures fabricated
Within those timeless hedgerows:
Pig shit here, cow-dung there, and
The sheep everywhere flung like
Khaki turtles in African kraals –
Indeed there were times when
The steering wheel slipped as if
Touched by vandaline anti-climb
And I suffered to share the spirited
Smells of the lovely dales with
Another, living from pillar to post.

It was after the coppers suddenly
Showed up in my mirror as you
Struggled to belt up, shivering from
The hangovers of your whisky and
Soda binges of yester weeks, you
Said, that the insufferable whiff
Of joint from your scruffy anorak
Began to bother – were the coppers
Really following you or was that
Your roundabout trap of getting
Me nicked for picking up the joint-
smoking hiker? So, when you chose
The front seat, Justine Copps, when
You wondered why this sojourner
You called Black Samaritan was
Deaf to your compliments after
God's people had ignored your

Pleading thumb – it's the coppers
I was nervous about. Was I relieved,
Therefore, when you yelled, 'Here,
This junction is home, Clapham
Village!' as the coppers drove past,
Happily, and I recalled an IRA bomb
Defused at London's Clapham Junction once.

Fallout from Our Iraq Wars on Oil

Now even our Vale of York is turning
Black or white; the grey we cherished
Once is no more and though the pigeons
Spread their wings on pavements for
Our pleasure cooing: *nguku nguku mcheche,*
Nguluche kutanjila, ndame kuwasala, though
Pheasants scratch at the winding tracks
Of Yorkshire Dales, the daffodils of our
Adopted Spring are beginning to falter.
Is it the fallout from our Iraq wars on oil
And the laws that threaten to turn radical
Frogs into terrorists that is out of joint?
Why do pigeons peck at the snow on my
Windowsill, cooing about flying away?

Nguku nguku mcheche, nguluche kutanjila, ndame kuwasala:
If I fly away, I am trapped; if I stay here, I'll die of hunger.

OF PRISONS THAT WON'T GO AWAY

The Stench of Porridge

(for Jeoff Thindwa)

Why does the stench of porridge
With maggots and weevils floating,
The scorching heat trapped
Within reeking walls,
The irritation of shrilling
Cicadas and centipedes at night,
The hyenas forever *hooing*,
The scorpion's ugly sting
Splitting down the spine,
Track us wherever we hide?
Why does the daily bending
At strip searches as prison
Guards hunt the anus for
Bogus designs of our escapes,
The monthly purging with
Malaria, cholera, diarrhoea,
The poison pigeon peas,
The Sick Bay queues of skeletal
Limbs craving for valium
To heal deadly silences –
Why does the stench of prison
Suddenly catch us like lust?
Didn't the spirit govern once for all,
The groans of prisoners dying next cell
The pangs of prisoners gone mad,
The weeping blisters on our elbows,
Knees, balls, buttocks, wherever
And the blizzards blustering
The rusty tin roofs
Where helpless chickens
Drip in the storm?
For how long does this
Stench intend to trail us?
Or is it really true what they say,
'Once prisoner always prisoner'.

It's the Speed That Matters, Dear Padre

(for Fr Pat O'Malley, Fr Leo Morahan & Landeg White)

It's the speed, dear padre, the speed with
Which you risk to save one's life that counts.

The chameleon hesitates, often three times,
Before putting his foot down, the squirrel

Lashes its bushy tail before it leaps onto its
Safer baobab branch, the spotted cheetah

Stalks the undergrowth, smarting for her
Final pounce, but nothing happens without

The speed with which they do their deed
My dear padre, the speed is all – for it was

The speed with which you chose to telephone
Speaking in Gaelic, so our tyrant's surrogates

Could not decipher your word – that you had
Seen this bumblebee chained behind their

Security van – it's the speed your Galway Parish
Friend sent the word to our friend in York

To shout to the world for another who'd been
Taken; it's the speed the radio waves recycled

The word across the globe the following day,
Shaming our Life Excellency and his minions,

Shattering their designs to kill; it's the speed
That saved the bumblebee. Even when you

Chose to bury the rebel's mother regardless,
Padre, alone, after University Registrar had

Dared any colleague to bury the rebel's mother,
It was the speed with which you slighted their

Pitiful fears, to minister to the dead as you must;
It's the speed to rescue that matters, dear padre.

On David Constantine's Poem

(for Landeg White, David Constantine & Co)

Your poem for Irina Ratushinskaya
On your birthday has reached these
Putrid African prison walls it
Was probably not meant for;
What cheer distant voices must bring
Another poet crackling in the Russian
Winters of icicle cells.
Yet even in this dungeon where
Day after day we fester within
The walls of the tropical summers
Of our Life President
And his hangers-on, even here,
What fresh blood flushes
When an unexpected poem arrives,
What fire, what energy
Inflames these fragile bones!
Indeed we have the verses in common,
Notwithstanding
The detention camps
The laws against poems
The black or white
Traitor or patriot
Binaries;
But secure in your
Voices of solidarity,
We'll crush the crocodiles
That crack our brittle bones.
Do not falter then, brother,
Do not waver, dear brethren,
But craft on the verses
Whose ceaseless whisper resonates
Beyond the Whitehalls of our dreams!

On Driving His Life Excellency's Political Enemies to Scarborough

(for Kanyama Chiume, David Rubadiri & Felix Mnthali)

And if you should wish me another prison let it be
For rallying within the city of York those rebels you

Could not stomach only weeks after our independence,
Seeking not their scholarly papers, but their learned

Memories of your wrath at the first cabinet and other
Crises you'll doubtless bequeath this tender nation.

And what a conference, what revelations, what cheer!
Did you really get struck off the medical register for

Consuming another man's assets, your own receptionist
Nurse, what is it about receptionist nurses with you? And

Those abortions in Ghana, did you thank the rhinoceros
Who summoned you to liberate your homeland instead?

What treason did you see in the moustache of your
Political enemy number one? What revolt in the verse

Of your UN envoy that we read hidden in our youthful
Blankets, and how dare you jail my teacher for being

Just another clever northerner? If you should invent
Another prison for me, let it be for driving your three

Political enemies to Scarborough one English summer
Afternoon, letting them relax to watch Scarborough

Children surfing with the seagulls and riding the tender
Crests and splashes of the calm bay; let it be for buying

Your rebels huge portions of Scarborough fish 'n' chips,
And sitting at the wooden table to analyse the songs your

Dancing witches sang to you; let it be for good reason
Not the conjectures of your mistress about my treason!

On U Win Tin's 75th Birthday (March 2005)

'U Win Tin, on this your seventy-fifth
birthday, we your jailors have the pleasure
to remind you that you are still being
held under Emergency Provisions Acts
bequeathed by the British. You are
still being accused of thinking, speaking
out, feeling and inciting others so to do.
You'll continue to be incarcerated for
promoting what you call freedom of speech
and we call sheltering traitors or those
likely so to be. We'll still condemn you
to sleep on cold concrete floors without
blankets or mats, alone or with others
in cells three paces by two. And should
you think, feel, speak out about these
or similar matters, we'll dump you in
solitary confinement cells again whether
your rotting teeth grind, your aching back
throbs or your eyesight begins to die.
And should you,
on this your seventy-fifth birthday, need
family for medication, food, warmth, we've
been directed by the powers that be to let
you have monthly family visits. Should
you try to smuggle out notes to your UN
friends and others outside these Burmese
islands, should we find, God forbid, after
our strip searches, you possess proscribed
effects like little radio sets, magazines, pens,
newspaper cuttings from overseas human
rights campaigns for your release, expect
thunderous crack down to strike you like
lighting. And should you attempt to smile,
laugh, sing, break wind, even accidentally,
to celebrate this your seventy-fifth birthday,
we your jailors will show you what bars
Insein Prison is capable of imposing on
fragile bones like yours. For, you U Win
Tin, are a shameless dissident, and another
notorious terrorist to their excellencies up
on high. And the war we are waging against
characters like you is total and we intend

to win, we swear by our security reasons!
So, there you have it, your position again
perfectly clarified, how do you plead now?'

Ken Saro-Wiwa's Pipe Still Puffing (Ten Years On)

Yesterday, I stopped at another
Shell petrol station and recalled how
you'd have loved to puff from your pipe
there, for your Ogoni people and land;
I did not, of course, stop to fill up with
petrol, definitely not! I stopped merely
to have a good pee, as promised I would
when they got you executed. Today, I
thought, well, why don't we treasure
the moment we once shared?

Altar-boy at Sixty

(a self-praise poem)

At sixty Altar-boy crossed himself:
at deum qui letificat juventutem meam
(to God who gives joy to my youth)
to venerate another annunciation
of the Blessed Virgin Mary and
celebrate his birthday; the smoking
sacristy wine he often sipped when
Father was not looking, the puffing
incense and the aroma of the candle
flames he loved to put out with his
fingers after mass, one by one, these
dilated his nostrils – even the seraphs
and cherubs chiselled into the altar
of Mulanje cedar aitchooed! What
at deum qui letificat juventutem meam!

The second youth emerged on sandy
beaches among the tattered loin-cloth
fishermen jumping into dugout canoes
to cast their net. Altar-boy recalled
how the spindly hands once hauled
ashore an angry crocodile tangled
in a fish-laden net and how the beast
lashed, lashed, lashed to liberate itself
from the taut net and anxious hands
as they tugged at their booty ashore,
together chanting, until a fishmonger
shoved reed blade past the creature's
windpipe choking it dead – ah, what
at deum qui letificat juventutem meam
boomed for hordes of fish to come!

And the third youth came drifting
on Milimbo Waters with his mates,
their cock-float raft pushing papyrus,
reed and grass, unsettling throngs of
mosquitoes in basins of green water
lilies and, with fishing rod in hand,
worms on hooks, the youths imagined
mums and sisters at home waiting for
their fish to pull. But when Altar-boy
spotted ripples blinking beside clusters
of reed and knew the monster poking

its nose above water ready to pounce –
what pole, what paddle, what hand
clap, the water, at once, splash! And
how the brute shot past as the youths
cracked their *at deum qui letificat juven-
tutem meam* in the blazing African sun.

But binning the romance at sixty, after
his friend had left for the warmth and
smoking vines of Portugal, Altar-boy
marvelled what the New Millennium
promised, beginning with his beloved
children, how they'd stunned his wife
and he with another menu of their Silver
Wedding Anniversary, dressed for hired
York city photographers; Fr Matthew
who'd married them in Africa flown in
from Amsterdam, from Dublin Fr Pat,
York Fr Austin O'Neill of Tang Hall
and scores of friends gathered for their
jubilee mass and dinner-dance at New
Earswick Folk Hall – and what *at deum
qui letificat juventutem meam* it became!

Altar-boy had begun by wondering
why at sixty he was suddenly so bold
about the memories he recalled, why
he began to speak in quotation marks.
He drove to Leeds; one of Africa's
laureates was giving the Reith Lecture
on dignity – how fragile bones survived
the humiliation the powerful inflicted,
as instanced by Yasser Arafat's Ramallah
children driven to wear explosives to
restore their dignity and youths from
Northern Ireland knee-capped; when
the poet's message seemed buried in
the usual audience ding-dong of Israel
versus Palestine, Altar-boy, painfully
asked what he would in times like these:
'But how does your swallow, caged in
suitcase after suitcase, leaping from port
to port, endure the indignities suffered
over the years?' No answer, not until
a glass of wine later, though even then
no *at deum qui letificat juventutem meam*!

Not after Liverpool Metropolitan
Cathedral even, where he read for
the best man of his Silver Wedding
Anniversary, who'd passed younger,
stubborn, causing colleagues, projects
in surgery and family to stumble in
mammoth quotation marks about
the kind of death they thought they
knew, not in that solemn ambience
did Altar-boy grasp what *at deum
quiletificat juventutem meam* confronts
family when their loving dad passes!
And when Michael Foot opened
Hazlitt's Exhibition at Dove Cottage
Altar-boy asked the idol of his London
University days why Her Majesty's
Leader of Opposition once defied
Maggie Thatcher's habit, wearing
his anti-nuclear war duffel coat, yet
placed his wreath at the cenotaph in
the ceaseless English drizzle – ah,
the *at deum qui letificat juventutem
meam* Thatcher bore thereafter!

Altar-boy recalled how exile had
begun with the sparrow; cast out
of the crocodile waters of home for
his twitterings, how sparrow had
crossed continents pecking at living
tales that would feed his chicks as
they flew beneath wings of hostile
currents, leaping among the frogs
of Leiden here, edging Cork city
scaffoldings there, until he perched
on the hills and valleys of Grasmere
there to part the bracken of Dove
Cottage, considering how the snails
in the undergrowth kept the bracken
glowing, come rainbow, come drizzle,
come blizzards of snow; Altar-boy
thought he might splash about Lake
Windermere to discover if crocodiles
defined lakes here too or to plunge
the crystal clear waters of Coniston
to cleanse his soul with the swarms
of minnows flirting their *at deum qui*

letificat juventutem meam at his feet, but
no pike's head showed up to greet him!

Yet wherever he turned and whatever
memories probed, Altar-boy wondered
what *at deum qui letificat juventutem meam*
he could really boast at sixty; he found
nothing 'to write home about', except
perhaps once filling his Grasmere bath-
tub, when he thought he had rescued
a spider – and what *at deum qui letificat*
juventutem meam that was for Altar-boy!

Can of Beasts Madonna Opened

Why must adopting an orphan
open another can of beasts for our
Christian claimed states? Which
mum traversing another country's
rolling mountains, craggy hills,
undulating terrain criss-crossed
by smiling lakes, laughing rivers,
tweeting streams, bubbling brooks,
until she encounters a whirlpool
of orphans; which mother moved
would not reach out for her purse
to buy tins of milk for the orphans
to survive, then want one to adopt
and save his life?

So, where does this can of
holier beasts originate, that must
vilify every little good done on
earth? And these culture-identity
crises we invent for this child, what
justice, what laws, what dignity
can mean beasts like you and me
truly restore, what's wrong with
celebrity if she can rescue human
life besides? Why don't we submit
honourably: the singer has beaten
us at our game, or do our learned
lawyers merely seek the crumbs
of her cake to share – whatever;
but what ironies, what jealousies
exposed, and what a brazen lot
of mindless beasts we must seem!

Do you remember the other
mum who left her breast-feeding
child in Nairobi to join the visiting
UN mission bound for Darfur, how
they landed in a vortex of emaciated
mothers and their skeletal children;
do you remember Sarah's blue eyes
locked into Nansi's brown eyes as
Nansi fed twins on dust-dry breasts;
how Sarah, tuned-in, left her UN
line, grabbed Nansi's skinny twins,
pulled her blouse, and offered each
twin each of her full nipples to suckle

to their hearts' content? Don't you
recall cameras from Sarah's colleagues
clicking for the big issue back home,
and aghast, chiding: why don't you
care about your own first, why must
you always offer your body to those
probable bearers of HIV/AIDS?

Stop wondering then
why adopting a child or offering full
breasts for gaunt twins to see another
day, is such a deadly sin; do not ask
why, for God's sake, it must be cool
to hold back, why a piece of justice,
a speck of instinctive gesture, a dash
of unreserved love for the novel must
be maligned, or doled out like soup
to the blistered lips of the hungry, do
not bother to enquire why we must
all befriend a spaniel, even sponsor
a hound at The Dogs' Trust instead –
in this land that purports to be just!

Retinal Screening, Christmas 2006

Anyone arrived for retinal screening?
Hands up. She picks her client like
A school teacher. Sits him on straight
Chair. Close left eye with left hand.
Which line can you read from my eye
Testing board? Tick. Now right eye
With right hand. You can read each
Letter in the last line? That must be
The eye we removed the cataract last
Time. So when Christmas comes she
Must monitor whatever grey his eyes
Have gathered. And hand out tissue
Hankies for her eye drop installation.
The trick, she finds, is to close eyes
After drops. And they'll fizz, sharp
At first, then warm – the drops that
Swell pupils before photographing
Inside the eye – the bit that's irksome.
Phase two. Sit in the waiting room
Before the photographer's reckoning,
Where the Christmas tree menaces
Yours at home whose evergreen apex
Star glints, branches draped in red,
Gold, sliver chains, bells, balls glisten.
Then the dark room. Place chin on
Little scoop of camera's stand. Lock
Left eye into camera. Do you see
The red line? Flash! Eye burns? Blurs?
It would, wouldn't it, first white blur,
Then blue, then white again. Right
Eye next, all the while concentrating
On the red line. Flash! Three blurs?
Done. Don't drive home yet; recover
Full sight in car park, where you hear
A hundred aeroplanes and Christmases
Are fogged out, you hear, which won't
Signify, as you marvel at the number
Of rituals that multiply each year.

NOTES

Beasts of Nalunga

In 2003, in Chief Chiwere's area, Dowa district, Central Malawi, mysterious beasts suddenly appeared in a village called Nalunga. Their origin was unknown. They were variously believed to be rabid hyenas, lions, leopards or cheetahs. And killed or maimed domestic animals and people, scattering them from their homes; in Nalunga village alone the papers estimated some 3,000 people abandoned their homes. Earlier, human like beasts had appeared in Chief cheSomba's area, Zomba district, Southern Malawi; these sucked people's blood in their sleep at night, apparently using intravenous tubes. The mystery surrounding these human/beast/vampire stories was the subject of singers and storytellers, some of whom compared the character of these beasts to that of the IMF, the World Bank and other profit-oriented multinational economic suckers that have no sympathy for human suffering. We exploited the tales of beasts of Nalunga and vampires of cheSomba in the creative writing workshops that I ran for the Malawi Writers' Union in the capital city.

But beasts and vampires have bothered people throughout the country from the time the British ruled Nyasaland Protectorate, perhaps even earlier. And during Hastings Banda's autocratic rule these blood-sucking creatures appeared in several townships in the country's southern and central regions. They became popularly associated with the enigmatic 'Chilobwe Murders'. Such blood-sucking creatures have fascinated historians and other academics; they have a puzzling cyclic temporal existence of their own. In her article, which appeared in 2003 in the 'Diary' section of the *London Review of Books*, Professor Megan Vaughan, now of Cambridge University, wrote informally about them.

The idea of corpses being taken to the grave through windows rather than the main door, as described in the poem, has an ancient origin. Tradition has it that coffins of people who took medicines in order to live long had to pass through windows rather than doors on their way to the cemetery; this ensured that, after their burial, such people did not turn into monsters that molested people in villages. The idea was originally inspired by a poem written by one early member of University of Malawi's writers' group, Swanzie Agnew, whose poem was about how ancient South African peoples buried their dead by leaving them on open mountain tops for the vultures to assault.

Banda's regime was sustained principally by three intelligences from the police, the army and the Malawi Young Pioneer Movement. The latter was further subdivided into 'spearheads', each purporting to spearhead the country's rural and urban development. The movement had spearhead for agriculture, spearhead for commercial business, spearhead air wing, spearhead intelligence, and a special spearhead music band (for the propagation of Banda-oriented local music). All of these had peace and calm, law and order as their motto, though brutality, violence and chaos is what they brought.

For the poem to be written at all grateful thanks to Asbjørn Eidhammer of the Norwegian Embassy in Malawi who introduced me to the newly formed Malawi Writers Union and asked me to run creative writing workshops with them in 2003. Many thanks also to the British Council for hosting the event in their Lilongwe premises. The visit gave me the opportunity to read from my own work in Lilongwe, Chancellor College Great Hall Zomba, Blantyre and Mzuzu – this was the first time ever that I had read in public in my own country!

This poem is dedicated to the memory of Anthony Nazombe, student, colleague, literary critic, poet, freedom-fighter, above all, my son's godfather. I enjoyed discussing the various sections of the poem when I visited him at Chirunga Campus, Zomba – his passing is greatly mourned.

The Patron of Jubilee 2000

Ujamaa is the philosophy of self-reliance in educational, economic, social and political development for the so-called 'third world' as propounded by Mwalimu Julius Nyerere, the first President of Tanzania. It is believed that the western world conspired to kill the philosophy because it excluded the capitalist approach to the solution of African problems; *harambee* – translates roughly as let's pull together, united.

Altar Boy at Sixty

This poem is dedicated to the memory of Dr Robert Woof, Director of the Wordsworth Trust, at Dove Cottage, Grasmere, Cumbria, with whom I shared the experiences described in the various sections. Robert invited me as poet in residence at Dove Cottage, where I stayed for three years and composed most of the poems in *Beasts of Nalunga*. He will remain a special friend for joining the many distinguished people who fought for my freedom from Banda's prison – he is deeply missed.